D1737748

Dinosaurs by Design

ARMORED DINOSAURS

RANKING THEIR SPEED, STRENGTH, AND SMARTS

MARK WEAKLAND

🌐 WORLD BOOK

This World Book edition of *Armored Dinosaurs:
Ranking Their Speed, Strength, and Smarts*
is published by agreement between
Black Rabbit Books and World Book, Inc.
© 2020 Black Rabbit Books,
2140 Howard Dr. West,
North Mankato, MN 56003 U.S.A.
World Book, Inc.,
180 North LaSalle St., Suite 900,
Chicago, IL 60601 U.S.A.

Jennifer Besel, editor; Catherine Cates, interior designer;
Grant Gould, cover designer; Omay Ayres, photo researcher

Library of Congress Control Number: 2018008172

ISBN: 978-0-7166-3932-9

Printed in the United States. 1/19

Image Credits
Alamy: Mohamad Haghani,
14–15; dinosaurpictures.org: Mar-
iana Ruiz, Cover (dino); Masato Hato-
ri: 11; Science Source: José Antonio Peñas,
6–7; Kurt Miller, 22–23; Shutterstock: 90miles,
21; Catmando, 20, 32; Herschel Hoffmeyer, 4–5
(both), 24 (dino); Kiarnight, 29 (Ankylosaurus); Mi-
chael Rosskothen, 16–17; Mirco Vacca, 1; mr.Timmi,
29 (Stegosaurus & Edmontonia); Naz-3D, 31; Quick
Shot, Cover (bkgd); Warpaint, 3, 8, 9, 24 (bkgd);
SuperStock: Stocktrek Images, 12, 19, 27
Every effort has been made to contact copyright
holders for material reproduced in this book.
Any omissions will be rectified in subse-
quent printings if notice is given
to the publisher.

CONTENTS

CHAPTER 1

Tough
Plant Eaters. 4

CHAPTER 2

Compare
the Dinos. 10

CHAPTER 3

Surviving
with Armor. 26

Other Resources. 30

TOUGH

Plant Eaters

An **armored** dinosaur munches a plant. Suddenly, a huge meat eater appears. It snaps its long, sharp teeth. But the armored dinosaur doesn't run. Instead, it swings its dangerous tail. Its sharp spikes are not a delicious sight.

Armored dinosaurs didn't need to run from **predators**. Thick bone plates covered their bodies. These animals weren't easy to eat.

Large and Heavy

Armored dinosaurs lived 170 to
65 million years ago. They were large
and heavy. Many crawled along on
short, powerful legs. Sitting low to the
ground protected their soft bellies.
Predators snapped at them. But sharp
teeth found only hard bone.

GROUPS OF ARMORED DINOSAURS

Armored dinosaurs can be placed into two groups. Each group has different features.

ANKYLOSAURIA
(ang-ky-luh-SAW-ree-uh)

spikes
across back

plates
on skin

clubbed tails
(on many)

round
skulls

short,
stout legs

Dinosaurs developed at different times. They **evolved** in different environments. These differences caused some to grow tails with clubs or spikes. Others did not.

STEGOSAURIA
(steg-oh-SAW-ree-uh)

narrow skulls

short front legs

plates or spikes down the back

spiked tails

CHAPTER 2

Compare the

Edmontonia

(ed-mon-TOHN-ee-uh)

This dinosaur lived in the woods of what is now North America. If a predator leaped on it, its **sturdy** legs pushed back hard. Sharp spikes stuck out from its shoulders. One **shrug** and a meat eater got a mouthful of painful points.

FEATURE FACTS

LENGTH	**13 to 23 FEET** (4 to 7 METERS)	**CLUBBED TAIL**
WEIGHT	**about 6,000 POUNDS** (2,722 KILOGRAMS)	**NO**

Some scientists
think Edmontonia
made honking
sounds.

Armored dinosaurs spent their days **grazing** on plants.
Some might have traveled in herds.

Polacanthus

(pol-uh-KAN-thus)

It's easy to see why this dinosaur's name means "many spines." Polacanthus moved slowly. A fast predator could run it down. But what meat eater would want to chomp on those spikes?

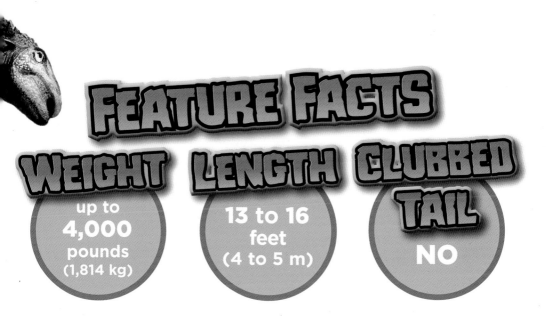

FEATURE FACTS

WEIGHT
up to
4,000
pounds
(1,814 kg)

LENGTH
13 to 16
feet
(4 to 5 m)

CLUBBED TAIL
NO

Euoplocephalus

(yu-oh-plo-SEF-ah-luss)

Scientists have found many **fossils** of Euoplocephalus. Its tail had a large club of bone. This dino would have whipped its tail. That motion would have forced enemies to run off.

FEATURE FACTS

		CLUBBED TAIL
LENGTH	**16 to 20 FEET** (5 to 6 M)	
WEIGHT	about **4,000 POUNDS** (1,814 KG)	**YES**

ARMORED DINOSAURS TIMELINE

STEGOSAURUS
156 to 144 million
years ago

KENTROSAURUS
155 to 150 million
years ago

POLACANTHUS
130 to 125 million
years ago

| MILLIONS OF YEARS AGO | 160 | 140 | 120 |

ANKYLOSAURUS
74 to 67 million
years ago

EDMONTONIA
73 to 70 million
years ago

TALARURUS
99 to 89 million
years ago

EUOPLOCEPHALUS
71 to 68 million
years ago

100   80   60

Stegosaurus

(steg-ah-SOR-us)

Like many armored dinosaurs, Stegosaurus was huge. Its body was the size of a truck. But its brain was small. To defeat smart meat eaters, Stegosaurus developed plates and spikes. It could not **outwit** a predator. But it could protect itself with armor.

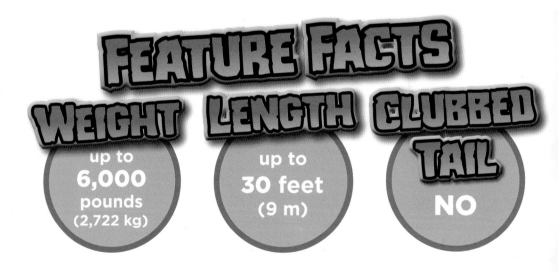

FEATURE FACTS

WEIGHT
up to
6,000
pounds
(2,722 kg)

LENGTH
up to
30 feet
(9 m)

CLUBBED TAIL
NO

Stegosaurus had a brain the size of an orange.

Kentrosaurus

(ken-TRO-sor-us)

Kentrosaurus fossils were found in present-day Africa. This dino swung its thick tail. It used its spikes to stab. A predator that was stabbed wouldn't want to keep fighting.

FEATURE FACTS

WEIGHT
about
4,000
pounds
(1,814 kg)

LENGTH
13 to 16
feet
(4 to 5 m)

CLUBBED TAIL
NO

Ankylosaurus

(an-KY-luh-sor-us)

Ankylosaurus was one of the largest armored dinosaurs. It was like a living tank. It did not have a gun or missile. But it did have a deadly tail club. And it had lots of armor. Even its eyelids were protected.

FEATURE FACTS

| LENGTH | 23 to 30 FEET (7 to 9 M) | CLUBBED TAIL |
| WEIGHT | about 8,000 POUNDS (3,629 KG) | YES |

What might have attacked Ankylosaurus? Tyrannosaurus rex was alive at the time. So was the fierce Tarbosaurus. But they would have had to be very hungry to take on a well-armored dinosaur.

Talarurus

(tah-la-RUR-us)

Scientists have found fossils of Talarurus in what is now Asia. A clump of bone tipped its tail. Spiky plates crossed its back and neck. This dino couldn't run fast. But it could spin quickly to attack with its tail.

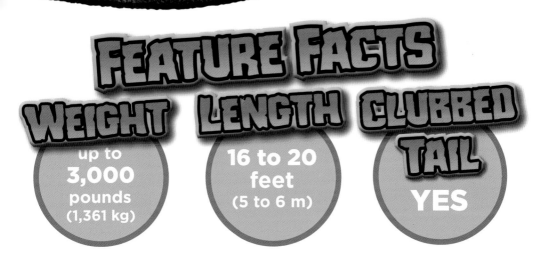

FEATURE FACTS

WEIGHT	LENGTH	CLUBBED TAIL
up to **3,000** pounds (1,361 kg)	**16 to 20** feet (5 to 6 m)	**YES**

CHAPTER 3

Surviving with

Armored dinosaurs were slow-moving plant eaters. They lived on Earth for millions of years. To survive, they grew armor that protected their bodies. They had spikes and clubs. And they had strong legs and tails. They might have been slow. But they were mighty.

COMPARE THEM!

Rank the dinos in this book. Then go find information on other armored dinos. How do they compare?

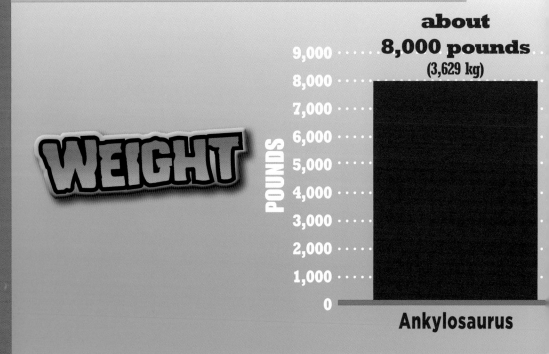

WEIGHT

about
8,000 pounds
(3,629 kg)

POUNDS

9,000
8,000
7,000
6,000
5,000
4,000
3,000
2,000
1,000
0

Ankylosaurus

CLUBBED TAIL

············► **NO**

Edmontonia
Kentrosaurus
Polacanthus
Stegosaurus

············► **YES**

Ankylosaurus
Euoplocephalus
Talarurus

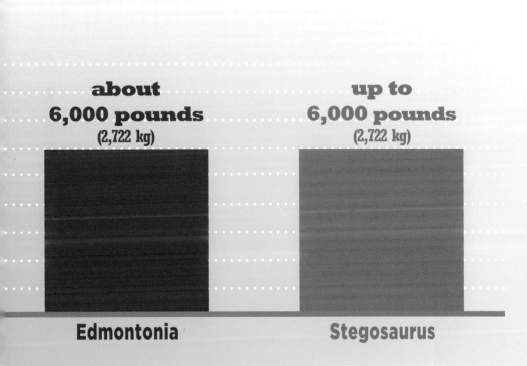

**about
6,000 pounds**
(2,722 kg)

**up to
6,000 pounds**
(2,722 kg)

Edmontonia

Stegosaurus

LENGTH

**Stegosaurus
up to 30 feet**
(9 m)

**Ankylosaurus
23 to 30 feet**
(7 to 9 m)

**Edmontonia
13 to 23 feet**
(4 to 7 m)

GLOSSARY

armored (AR-muhrd)—having a protective outer layer

evolve (ih-VOLV)—to slowly change

fossil (FAH-sul)—the remains or traces of plants and animals that are preserved as rock

graze (GRAYZ)—to feed on growing grass or herbs

outwit (owt-WIT)—to get the better of someone or something by being more clever

predator (PRED-uh-tuhr)—an animal that eats other animals

shrug (SHRUG)—to raise or draw in the shoulders

stout (STOWT)—large, round, and bulky

sturdy (STUR-dee)—strong and healthy

BOOKS

Carr, Aaron. *Ankylosaurus.* Dinosaurs. New York: Smartbook Media Inc., 2018.

Peterson, Megan Cooley. *The Dinosaur Extinction: What Really Happened?* History's Mysteries. Mankato, MN: Black Rabbit Books, 2019.

Waxman, Laura Hamilton. *Discovering Stegosaurus.* Dinosaurs. Mankato, MN: Amicus, 2019.

WEBSITES

Armored Dinosaurs
www.kidsdinos.com/armored-dinosaur/

Dinosaurs
discoverymindblown.com/category/dinosaurs/

Prehistoric World
www.nationalgeographic.com/science/the-prehistoric-world/

A

Ankylosaurus, 17, 22, 23, 28–29

E

Edmontonia, 10, 11, 17, 28–29

Euoplocephalus, 14, 15, 17, 28

G

groups of armored dinosaurs, 8–9

K

Kentrosaurus, 16, 21, 28

P

Polacanthus, 13, 16, 28

S

Stegosaurus, 16, 18, 19, 28–29

T

Talarurus, 17, 25, 28